NINJA WARRIOR

BOJUTSU DEFENSE TECHNIQUES

JACK HOBAN

CONTEMPORARY
BOOKS, INC.
CHICAGO ▪ NEW YORK

Library of Congress Cataloging-in-Publication Data

Hoban, Jack.
    Ninja warrior.

    1. Stick fighting.   I. Title.
GV1141.H62   1987   796.8   87-20091
ISBN 0-8092-4726-7

Published by Contemporary Books, Inc.
180 North Michigan Avenue, Chicago, Illinois 60601
Manufactured in the United States of America
International Standard Book Number: 0-8092-4726-7

Published simultaneously in Canada by Beaverbooks, Ltd.
195 Allstate Parkway, Valleywood Business Park
Markham, Ontario L3R 4T8 Canada

Contents

Acknowledgments

S ince my study is an ongoing process, this list gets longer every day! But for now, let me thank Dr. Ken Cassie: photographer, linguist, and ocean swimmer extraordinaire. Ken Lux, Victor Acevedo Ramirez, Norman Flam, and Mildred Flam for lending me their bodies and for being very good friends. Wendy, for her patience. And, of course, Dr. Masaaki Hatsumi. Domo arigato goziamasu.

Foreword
by Stephen K.
Hayes

This latest book by Jack Hoban is a perfect follow-up to his previous book on knife defenses. In *Ninja Warrior: Bojutsu Defense Techniques*, he expands on his presentation of the philosophies for dealing with fights in a manner which is easily grasped and immediately useful. This volume contains numerous real-life combat scenarios, but it is perhaps the conduct and life strategy of the contemporary ninja warrior that is most pointedly illustrated.

Jack attacks at the same time the two most extreme forms of misunderstanding that have grown over the past several years about training in the ninja warrior arts. On one hand, Jack confronts the dry technicians who have a little knowledge of the basics but none of the depth to bring the teachings to life. These characters would have their followers ignore the richness of our ninjutsu legacy as a thriving and relevant way of living. On the other hand, Jack exposes the irrational tendencies of the mysteriously inclined, who seem

overly attracted to the esoteric tradition that makes up
a part of the roots of the art. These characters would
foster in their followers the very irrationality that actually breeds the ignorance that the enlightened warrior
trains to combat.

This philosophy of balanced living through an em-
phasis on personal awareness and responsibility is
woven subtly into this book, which is ostensibly a
volume on using the stick as a self-protection tool. The
stick-fighting tradition of the ageless ninja legacy is
rich with significance, and Jack's book brings it into an
appropriately modern perspective in a very readable
manner. Though the exercises contained here are part
of a very old tradition, the thought-provoking training
tips and fighting scenarios are presented in a way that
emphasizes their freshness and newness as well.

Though few of us will have cause to employ the ninja
stick-fighting method in everyday life, we are all occa-
sionally subjected to other less tangible (and therefore
more difficult to identify and crush) forms of mental,
economic, and spiritual attack. For that reason, Jack
Hoban's interweaving of technique and philosophy,
strategy and application, make this book a great one for
the personal library of anyone fascinated by the usable
legacy of Japan's phantom warriors.

Introduction
Bojutsu and Ninpo
Taijutsu

The art of ninjutsu contains a broad range of stick-fighting (bojutsu) and other related arts. They include: yarijutsu (lance), kenjutsu (sword), juttejutsu (truncheon), tesson (iron fan), naginatajutsu (medium halberd), bisentojutsu (battle halberd), and others. My policy in a book such as this is to present the most useful applications of ninjutsu; the reader will find that most of the techniques illustrated herein utilize a hanbo, or three-foot stick. The generic word "bojutsu" usually refers to a standard six-foot staff. The word "han" therefore applies to a stick that is roughly half that size.

Keep in mind that, though the "traditional" hanbo (if it can be said that there was such a thing) was 2 feet 11¾ inches long and 1¹⁄₁₆ inch in diameter, you should use a stick that fits you. Experiment until you find the size that feels right. Then, make sure that you do not become locked into using that stick and that stick only.

I used the hanbo for obvious reasons, primarily because the size is in the same general category as a baseball bat, tire iron, or walking cane. If the trained practitioner must carry a weapon, the walking cane size is relatively unobtrusive. Chapter 5 does contain a brief introduction to long staffs as well as much shorter sticks.*

Although I do not dwell on the rokushaku bo (six-foot staff) in this book, I believe that the experienced practitioner should include some long bo training in his regimen for two reasons: 1) One may indeed encounter a weapon of this size: a rake or a shovel, for instance; and 2) the added length serves as an excellent training tool, in that the person using it must exaggerate the taijutsu body movement. It is very difficult to manipulate such a heavy weapon without employing the entire body, as the word taijutsu suggests. As the reader may know, the word taijutsu means "body art"; it implies that the practitioner has adopted a philosophy of full and natural body movement as a combat strategy.

As stated before, there are many traditional ways of employing the stick and other similar weapons. My purpose is to present training scenarios which correspond, in my opinion, to those that one is likely to encounter in the present day. Therefore, some of the more classical movements have not been included in this volume. They exist, of course, and can be learned from several of the senior Shihan of Masaaki Hatsumi's Bujinkan dojo. Dr. Hatsumi is the present Soke (grandmaster) of Kukishin Ryu, from whence this method of stick fighting originates.

A popular misconception that I would like to address at the start is that all weapon employment in ninjutsu is taijutsu with a weapon in one's hand. To an *extent* that is true. Our philosophy leads us to believe that movement of all kinds should be based upon *natural* ways of using the body, i.e. taijutsu. Unfortunately, for the practitioner to take full advantage of the 800 years of

---

*These short-stick techniques were originally tessen-jutsu techniques.

The author being disarmed by sensei Masaaki Hatsumi.

experience and lessons embodied in the Bujinkan Dojo, he or she must study the tactics and strategies of each individual weapon. Too often I have seen practitioners who have good backgrounds in taijutsu pick up a weapon and be only marginally effective with it, *or injure themselves*, because they have little experience with the idiosyncracies of the particular weapon. Therefore the adage "Ninja weapon fighting is taijutsu with a weapon in one's hand" is not entirely true. Additional training is required.

As far as the practicalities of stick fighting go, I am very excited about this book. It has given me the opportunity to address situations where innocent persons (including the elderly) can make do with a common article, even a cane or umbrella, when confronted by an assailant. It also gives me a chance to reintroduce my favorite subject: taijutsu. Indeed, as you become more natural in your movements, you will find the techniques quite easy and common sensical. You will also find that your occasion to require an overt self-protective act will all but disappear. This is the true magic of Ninpo.

The principles to be discussed are physical, intellectual, and emotional. Primarily, there are certain fundamentals of distance timing and technique that must be mastered to be totally proficient in this art. That takes practice; merely reading this book will not do it. Most importantly, however, the ability to hit something with a stick, and the facility for not being there when the stick travels to hit you, is paramount. Chapters 2 and 6 are devoted to these concepts. They cannot be overstressed. They are usually taken for granted (in the case of striking) and glossed over (in the case of avoiding). Let me say that striking effectively with a stick is not as easy as it sounds. Avoiding a strike with a stick is not as difficult as it sounds. They both, however, take practice.

Second, one must have some experience with different strategies for using self-protection and situational weapons. In Chapter 7, we will discuss a very possible fight scenario and some provisional weapons. It is up to you to learn the idiosyncracies of these and any other tool that you may have to employ.

Finally, this book deals with the emotional and philosophical aspects of self-protection and bojutsu. I suggest that you review my previous book, *Tantojutsu,* if you are totally unfamiliar with my philosophy of tying together the emotional and physical aspects of a fight. If you just need a quick reminder, it is in Chapter 1 of this volume. Do not gloss over this aspect of the training. Physical and intellectual preparation for a life-threatening situation is incomplete without the emotional preparation. If you cannot function in a situation which is most frightening and most bewildering from an emotional standpoint, what you *know* and what you *can* do may never become a factor. You may "short-circuit" before you can do anything. I will discuss the philosophy of self-preservation in Chapter 7 as well, but please use the emotional suggestions contained herein and in *Tantojutsu* as a way to add realism to your training.

Training should be done with a sympathetic partner. The Bujinkan training method is designed to be most effective for a person who is looking for a way to protect himself that is on a higher level than an animal's crude struggle for survival in a hostile world. Most of us have come from power- or speed-oriented systems. We have come to realize that these methods are not the way of the enlightened warrior who protects himself effortlessly. I assume that the people who are interested in the philosophy of Ninpo are already assured of their basic ability to protect themselves. They know that, if attacked, they could do *something* to protect themselves. Our training method is inappropriate for those inexperienced individuals who require competition and contention to prove to themselves that they are capable of defending themselves.

The Bujinkan training method consists of slow, deliberate movements that can be *gradually* heightened in speed and intensity as the process evolves. *Any* training technique that requires speed, force, or effort should be slowed down and reattempted without power and with an awareness of the strategic and philosophical opportunities that present themselves during the course of the clash. In other words: *train slowly* until you can recognize obvious flaws in the attacker's movement profile that you can use to lead him or her to defeat. *They are there, they do not require strength or power to exploit!*

Speed is meaningless in an encounter, anyway. It is the rhythm of the fight that is important. So many times I have seen people, who insist on training at "realistic" speeds, never gain a feeling for this most important element. Usually what happens is that the training attacker executes his or her attack in semi-slow motion while the defender frantically tries to complete a myriad of complicated and preconceived techniques. Afraid of injury, the assailant gives only a shell of a real attack, with dynamics that in no way resemble the real thing.

The best training is when the dynamics of the fight are real, regardless of the speed. The attacker attacks with the intent and movements that are as close as possible to the real thing (this takes a very talented training partner) but slowed down. The defender works at blending his movements with the attacker. In other words, he or she matches rhythm, not speed. As the abilities of the training partners progress, the speed can increase, but only at a rate equal to the defender's ability to continue blending with the attack.

If you will imagine a VCR with a slow-motion potentiometer, you can appreciate this analogy. If you slow the picture down, you expect *everything* to slow down together. This is how I'd like you to try your training. As you improve your ability to match the relative speed and intensity of the attacker, you will find that the speed is a minor detail.

Now speed the VCR up to real time or *any* time. The rhythm of the fight is the same. More will be said about this in Chapter 1. For now, please have an open mind, do not be afraid, and train for your own enjoyment, for it is fun to be safe, happy, and free.

NINJA WARRIOR

1
Fundamentals

It is very difficult for me to write a chapter on fundamentals without including a weave of philosophy and strategy. Indeed, what distinguishes the ninja combat method from all others is the unique perspective of the ninja. I will leave it to the reader to put the contents of this book into a personal perspective, as I have spent many years trying to do myself. Some of the fundamentals, of course, are very physical. Some of them will sound very philosophical, if not political. I cannot apologize for that. In the heart of the warrior such distinctions blur and have little meaning. I will, however, try to make my comments useful, rather than merely thought-provoking.

It has been said that one must fight with a stick as if it were a piece of rope. This has always been a difficult concept for me to accept literally. Yet, after gaining a certain comfort and facility with stick-fighting techniques, you may find that the stick becomes more than just a dead piece of wood. Certainly, it is a tool used

1

toward the end of the user; but it is, to a certain extent perhaps, a partner, also. We must always remember, however, that the individual who wields the stick retains ultimate responsibility for the good or bad that results. The important thing to realize is that the stick is a limited partner in the manifested action. It is an extension of the taijutsu skills of the user.

The same fundamentals that are present in unarmed taijutsu skills apply to stick fighting—only more so. A person with rudimentary skills exaggerates his inabilities when his techniques are enlarged by the employment of a weapon. This is why many instructors teach weapons only to the more advanced students.

The reservation of weapons training to the select advanced students is unnecessary in a non-competitive atmosphere. However, the training should be slow and deliberate, and the training atmosphere must be supportive and cooperative. Certain fundamental outlooks are vital, particularly if you must practice alone.

- Learn to do the techniques correctly as well as powerfully.
- Learn to be correct by becoming attentive to how your body moves in confluence with the strategy of the technique.
- Learn power the same way—by understanding how power is generated by the natural movement of your body.
- Do not fight instinctively, like an animal, but with your total human self: heart, mind, and body.
- Do not fight with brute strength, like an animal, but with the power that is generated by correct action.

I realize that these things are hard to understand, at first. Keep going. For now, let us work, initially, on the physical aspects of taijutsu that will support your stick-fighting training.

I believe that correct strategies of fighting result spontaneously from inside the person, not from a memorized list. The problem is that the emotions are so constricted by artificial sociological gunk, that what eventually is allowed to seep out does not at all resemble the highest level of human ability. Enlightened warriorship results from the ability to use only clear, uninhibited human values as a basis of action. In my earlier book, I presented certain exercises that I believe will help a person clarify his or her emotions so that the actions that flow from them will be just as clear and unfettered. I called these clarified emotions *whole-body attitudes.*

STANDING FIRM

In the standing-firm attitude we are aware of our own human right to protect ourselves against those who would harm us. We are firm in our knowledge that we

Shizen no kamae.

can handle the situation. This knowledge may be en-
hanced by the observation that we are obviously more
skilled than our opponent. The feeling is not unlike that
conveyed by a general as he enters his staff meeting.
You exude a solidness and certainty about the outcome
of what is happening. The feeling manifests itself, physically, in a natural posture that conveys your confi-
dence. Knees are relaxed, the breath is deep and full.
Feel yourself centered at the base of the buttocks. The
gaze is clear and steady.

RESPONSIVENESS

This attitude conveys that we, as humans, have a right
to be incomplete. We may be in a position of weakness,
due to a lack of physical strength, preparation, or
knowledge. The feeling is that queasiness in the pit of
the stomach that we have all experienced when we have
been intimidated in some way. Our natural reaction is
to move away from that which is attacking us. To
assume the attitude in the photograph, start from the
shizen no kamae and fall back to this defensive position,
leading with the abdomen. The back is straight, the
gaze is watchful, and the body and breath are centered
in the abdomen.

COMMITMENT

This attitude conveys that humans must be motivated
by reason. We act upon certain presituational values
that give a rightness to those actions. The feeling is a
joyous certainty in what must be done. Our tendency is
to embrace the activity without reservation. No offen-
sive attitude is rational without this motivation. To
assume the attitude in this picture, begin with the
shizen no kamae, allow the tool of your intention (in this
case, the hanbo) to lead you into action. Your gaze,
indeed your entire awareness, is focused. Do not con-

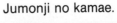

Jumonji no kamae.

Ichimonji no kamae.

fuse this focus with the flat focus usually referred to in martial arts, such as "two inches behind the target," etc. This is the three-dimensional focus of a laser beam that goes through the target to infinity. The body must not be tensed. The breath must come from the solar plexus.

AVOIDANCE

This attitude is a manifestation of a human's right to choose to avoid that which he feels is harmful to him. In this case, of course, it is an attack against one's person. The feeling can take many countenances: boredom, impatience, even a benevolent patronage. In my life, the feeling has come as a quiet disgust with the situation. You feel that you want it to end. You want as little to do with the situation, in terms of active participation, as possible. You are light on your feet, you are gazing at the larger picture, your breath is light and high.

Of course, there will probably never be a situation that fits any one of these moods perfectly. These definitions are for your training only: a way to clarify your own value system. I believe that once you know yourself, you can trust in your own self-protection abilities. If you have ever been in a critical or life-threatening situation, you know that it is very hard to define just

Hira ichimonji no kamae.

what it is that prompts action. You seem to move without thinking.

There is a lot of talk about "moving without thinking" in the more esoteric discussions of the martial arts. In a way, there is some truth to the statement "move without thinking." In other ways, what really happens could not be farther from "thoughtless." What happens is that you cannot *react*. You have no time to consciously evaluate the situation, search in your memory banks for the textbook solution to the problem, and then execute. What you do in that situation will be based upon certain presituational values that you have learned in your life. These values may be true or flawed, depending on your experiences, on what you have been taught by others, or by your training.

An involved discussion of such personal value systems is inappropriate for a book such as this. The one thing that I can do is to present a basic model of how the physical, emotional, and philosophical aspects of ninpo combine to suggest how this knowledge can be gained. This epistemology is my own and has been gleaned through my personal observations and study. I include it for your information only. I cannot say that is the official ninja philosophy, although I have come to see these things after studying taijutsu and the philosophies of many Eastern and Western sages and fools.

Physical	**Emotional**	**Philosophical**
Earth	Firmness	Sacredness of the Individual
Water	Responsiveness	Incompleteness of the Individual
Fire	Commitment	Reason
Wind	Avoidance	Choice
Void	Beyond Emotions	The Individual Acts with God

It is obvious that I have included a category, beyond emotions, that is not in *Tantojutsu*, per se, or elaborated upon above. Yet the void (as in devoid of a preconceived manifestation but not devoid of presituational logic) is a theme that must run through everything that we talk about in this book. If the other four "attitudes" are the ones that we try to clarify as we train, the void is the attitude that we *will* have when we actually act in the world.

Let us turn, finally, to body dynamics and the actual manipulation of the weapon. Here are some points to keep in mind as we proceed through this book and you try the actual techniques.

Relax. Probably the most difficult thing to do when learning something new is to relax and let it sink in. I consider myself fairly experienced in the martial arts. Most people, including myself, can be rather smooth when they are working off of their own energy. But most of us, including me, have a tendency to stiffen up when trying to imitate someone else's technique or someone else's energy. Keep in mind that you will be trying to imitate what *my* energy led *me* to do when the assailant in the photographs attacked me. It will feel odd to copy it exactly. Don't try. Look for the generic principle behind the technique and try to develop your own flow. Don't worry if it doesn't look exactly the same.

Fight with your whole body. Since you have a weapon in your hands, you will feel a tendency to focus your whole attention upon it. This is bad for two reasons. First, the stick does nothing without you. To be most effective, what you do should be done with your entire body, not just with the hand or arm that holds the stick. Second, you may ignore your other weapons, i.e. your other hand, elbows, legs, etc.

Hold the weapon loosely in your hand. Don't choke the stick! I once was told to hold a stick like a bird: too hard and you kill it; too soft and it will fly away. Allow the weapon to slide through your hands, allowing you to fine tune distance and timing, affording you the

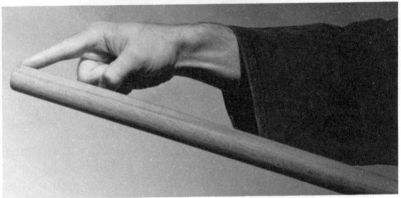

opportunity for complete flexibility in the fight. Secure the weapon only at the precise moment of impact—then relax your grip once more.

Use the tip of the stick to strike. When striking with the stick, practice your distancing so that the last half-inch or so strikes the target. Hit through the stick. What I mean by that is: focus through the target. I always imagine that my energy is flowing through the stick and out the end, like the laser beam focusing.

To see if you are following this principle, construct this experiment: after the strike, move the target out of the way. You should be pointing at and focusing through where the target was, rather than behind your back (like a baseball bat) or somewhere else.

Use your legs, not arms, to get your distance. Westerners have a tendency to be upper-body-oriented. That makes us want to reach with our arms, rather than move to the point where we must be in relationship to our opponent for maximum effectiveness. I have found that the most natural position for striking to be the one pictured here. The body is straight from the back foot to the head. The stick points straight at the target. The arms are held in a natural manner. The grip on the stick is mild. If you are too close or too far from the target, that is a job for your legs. Try to make only minor adjustments with your arms, remembering that each limb is responsible for your natural taijutsu power.

Most of the suggestions above are for hitting with a stick. Suggestions about grappling with a stick and avoiding the strike will come in later chapters. I believe that you will get an opportunity to strike at least one blow if you are confronted by an assailant. Will that hit be effective and serve to protect you? That is the topic of the next chapter.

2
Striking Methods

This chapter presents basic striking methods, including holding the stick and presenting some basic footwork. Additionally, we will discuss some training methods for learning how to hit with taijutsu power and the accuracy that will result.

It has always been interesting to me that many people want to learn all types of exotic techniques with the stick, but never show an interest in how to hit with it. Perhaps they take that ability for granted. After all, what Westerner has not hit something with a stick; if nothing else, at least a baseball? As you have seen and will see, however, the ninja method for hitting with a stick has little to do with the wind-up baseball way.

There is no question that you probably can hit hard with a slugger's swing. We have all seen the impressive results at the ballpark. But think about it. Aren't you ready and waiting for the ball? Aren't you much bigger than the ball? Will the ball try to counterattack? Of course, a baseball bat to a vulnerable part of the body will do a lot of damage; but be open-minded. The method of swinging a bat was designed for a specific purpose. The methods that you are about to see were developed long before the advent of baseball. They were designed and developed for the purpose of striking a human being or an attacking animal. Give them a try without allowing preconceptions to get in the way.

The final thing that I need to say before we get started is that power will be generated in two ways. The first way is by a whole-body attitude. Your whole body strikes the blow. The body is reacting naturally to the emotions that drive it. Philosophically, there is a correctness to the action which serves to give a spiritual resolve to the outcome. Beneath all that mumbo jumbo lies the fact that your body, when used naturally and without tension, supplies most of the power you will need to defend yourself. Your opponent will supply the rest.

Second, your opponent is attacking you. This is a seemingly strong but very negative power that can be turned back against itself. Mechanically, it will be your distancing and timing that forces the assailant to, literally, run into the stick and injure himself.

I like to think of it as good overcoming evil, or the unnatural being overcome by the natural. I don't want to get overly philosophical here, but recognize that a person who attacks you is wrong; you are right to defend yourself. There is power in that.

For now, let's look at the mechanics of hanbojutsu, as it pertains to striking.

The picture opposite shows the hira ichimonji no kamae (primary open) attitude. It is a neutral, rather inoffensive attitude. For our first strike, we will allow the stick to slide through our hands straight to the target. The stick remains roughly parallel to the ground. The body stays naturally straight through the entire movement. Notice the position of the hands, arms, legs, and feet.

The important feature of this strike is that there is no

wind-up. One can go from the natural position to the strike without wasted motion of any kind. The legs and body weight supply more power than an arm can. All of the power is directed through the target, rather than across it, like a baseball swing.

The following series of photographs show how this strike can be delivered at any angle. Keep in mind that either hand can be leading. You should practice both ways—right and left.

Continued on next page . . .

Of course, there are more than these directions from which to hit. You can hit from any number of angles. Eight is a good number to begin with. After practicing with these you will be good from any angle.

A ninth hit from this attitude is a stab. The tip goes straight to the target. Twist the stick with your right wrist in a clockwise (to you) direction. Coordinate the movement with the thrust or poke. This double action makes the strike both painful and powerful. Have a friendly training partner do it to you lightly, if you dare. Feels great, doesn't it?

The next series of strikes comes from the ichimonji no kamae. They are identical to the ones we have seen except for the attitude, which is responsive in nature. Although there will not be a series of pictures in this attitude, practice your strikes from every angle, as well.

The important thing about this attitude is the move backward. Use a 45-degree angle and don't step. Imagine that you are being pulled from the waist. The rest of the body follows because it is attached and must go. Your weight settles as you strike. This settling provides the grounded power for the hit.

The next strike is from the shizen no kamae. This is a particularly good attitude. As you can see, it looks like the unassuming pose of a person with a cane or umbrella. To strike, lead with the tip of the cane. For this exercise, step out at a 45-degree angle, and use your body dynamics, rather than your arm strength, to create power.

A fun and instructive way to practice this attitude by yourself is by doing figure eights. This is not only a wrist exercise, so remember to keep your feet moving.

On pages 24 and 25 is a stab technique from this attitude.

The stab technique from the shizen no kamae.

Finally, let's look at the follow-up strike from this attitude with some variations.

Obviously, there are many other ways to hit with the stick. You will see some others incorporated in the strategy and technique section in Chapter 3. I also suggest that you hit something besides air when you practice these strikes. You can practice against your partner's stick as shown on pages 28 and 29 or against a heavy bag.

As mentioned, hitting with a stick is not as easy as it sounds. You should practice a great deal. Don't assume that the target will be stationary, either. It won't be. That is where taijutsu comes in. You would like to strike from a position of strength—that is, you want to have the body dynamics that are roughly similar to the examples I've provided. The problem, however, is how to get the attacker to be at that half-inch area at the end of your stick. You will have to be able to judge the distance and timing of the attack and instantaneously move yourself so that the crucial half-inch is where it has to be for ultimate effectiveness. This is a skill that is not learned overnight. Be patient and keep training!

3
Four Stick-Fighting Strategies

E ach of the next four sections presents a strategy of stick fighting that generally corresponds to the attitudes we discussed in the fundamentals chapter. Keep in mind that these attitudes are in *you*, not in the techniques themselves. You must be in accord with the feeling of the technique for it to seem appropriate. In other words, when you do a standing-firm technique, you should have a standing-firm attitude, or it will feel unnatural. The same holds true for the other techniques and attitudes.

Along with that, you may see the defender in the photographs using many different striking and taijutsu techniques, none of which, you should understand, are particularly of one attitude or another. Try the techniques slowly, have a good training partner to help you (preferably a trusted friend) and relax.

Finally, don't worry about copying these techniques exactly as shown. There is no way that you will ever be in the exact same situation as the people in the photographs. A rule of thumb in this training method is: Don't try to learn the techniques; learn *from* the techniques.

Standing-Firm Technique 1:
Defense Against a Straight Punch

The attacker attempts a right-hand punch. The defender moves from shizen no kamae to plant the tip of the stick against the breastbone of the attacker. Bending the knees, the defender leans against the attacker's attacking arm with the other end of the stick, knocking him off balance. The defender knocks the attacker to the ground with a strike to the head with the right tip of the stick.

Remember what I said about rhythm. What happens between the photos is just as important as what happens in them. Start slow and learn to flow. If your distances are different than mine, walk over to where they feel more natural.

Continued on next page . . .

Standing-Firm Technique 2:
Defense Against a Front Kick

The attacker attempts a front kick, which the defender blocks by bending his knees. He then rises and counter- attacks with the right tip of the stick. To end the conflict, he squats once more and performs a sweep of the injured leg.

Be sure to keep your back straight; lift and lower the stick with your legs, as you would a heavy weight.

Standing-Firm Technique 3:
Defense Against a Stick

The attacker attempts an overhead strike with a stick. The defender shifts slightly to the outside of the strike from the shizen no kamae. He simultaneously lifts the stick up into the bottom of the attacking wrist. He follows up immediately with an overhand strike of his own. A continuation of his body motion allows him to counterattack to the head.

The standing-firm techniques will feel most natural if you are able to maintain a solid, no-nonsense attitude. If you cannot maintain that attitude, you can expect to feel that the whole strategy behind the technique is wrong; you will be correct. The techniques must flow from your attitude.

Responsive Technique 1:
Defense Against a Punch
The attacker attempts a straight punch to the face. From the hira no kamae, the defender drops back to the ichimonji no kamae, striking the inside of the attacker's wrist. With hip movement supplying the power, the defender reverses the stick and strikes the upper portion of the arm. He then continues the action and applies a choke to take the assailant to the ground.

Responsive Technique 2:
Defense Against a Stick

The attacker strikes straight down at the defender's head. The defender cuts to the outside and strikes the assailant in the ribs. He then rocks back in, grabs the attacking wrist and applies an elbow lock. Lastly, the defender pulls the attacker to the ground and immobilizes him.

Responsive Technique 3:
Defense Against a Knife
The attacker swipes at the eyes of the defender, who falls back and catches the wrist of the attacker. Using the forward momentum supplied by the legs, not the arms, the defender throws the assailant back. (Note that the knife may fly at this point, so be careful.) Use the follow-up strike or immobilization movement of your choice, at this point.

The secret to the responsive techniques will be found in the legs and feet, not in the arms. Look through the photos again, and look only at the lower half of the body. Also, feel free to experiment with the techniques. Mix and match different beginnings and endings. Follow up with a strike this time, try an immobilization the next time.

Committed Technique 1:
Defense Against a Punch

The attacker throws a roundhouse punch to the face. The defender attacks the biceps, dropping the attacker to the ground. He slips the end of the stick behind the arm and kneels on the elbow for immobilization.

45

Committed Technique 2:
Defense Against a Kick
The attacker throws a snap kick at the defender, who
moves forward at a 45-degree angle to the outside of the
kick. Since the defender was in hira ichimonji no
kamae, it is a simple and natural movement that puts
the point of the stick into the temple of the assailant.
Try this follow-up.

Committed Technique 3:
Defense Against a Knife

The attacker attempts an overhead stab at the defender, who swings the stick up into the shoulder of the assailant from shizen no kamae. He then grabs the attacker's wrist and pushes it back and away from the attacker's body. He is simultaneously sliding the stick behind the defender's back so that he will fall on it. He then pins the biceps for the immobilization.

These committed techniques require the defender actually to attack the attacker. Obviously, this is not always the easiest thing to do, so keep that in perspective. Yet, if you can make the techniques work, you may begin to discover the amount of power that you can summon up by the strength of your committed intention. There are also some moral questions that should be addressed. Is it ethical to attack? Even in self-defense? Obviously, I think so. Make sure that you have explored your own feelings before you try to use this attitude as a method of self-defense.

In a more technical vein, the power in these techniques comes from the legs and the taijutsu body movement. Do not use the strength of your arms to fight, put the stick where it has to be, and then use the rest of your body to supply the power.

49

Avoidance Technique 1:
Defense Against a Punch

The attacker throws a straight body punch. The defender slips to the inside and plants the stick into the attacker's ribs. He then punches with the right hand, reaches over the arm to grab the end of the stick, and applies a painful arm bar which can be used to lower the assailant to the ground.

Avoidance Technique 2:
Defense Against a Stick

The attacker swings with a baseball bat motion against the head of the defender, who slips inside the arc of the strike. Squatting, he slams the stick into the inside of the knee of the attacker, knocking him to the ground, where he can be pinned across the shin.

Avoidance Technique 3:
Defense Against a Knife
The attacker slices at the body of the defender, who slips inside the arc of the cut, catches the attacking wrist, then leans back against it to take the attacker to the ground. He steps on the wrist and brings the right end of the stick up for a slam to the head.

In the techniques above I talk about "slipping inside the arc of the strike or cut." Easier said than done, you might say. But believe me, it is easier than trying to block a knife slash. It is better to get out of the way. My suggestion is to move from the knees and ankles with a gliding motion. Don't hop around on stilt legs.

This entire chapter was designed to inspire more than instruct. There is no way that we can present every possible attack combination. The attitude that you adopt in a real situation should be devoid of all preconceptions, but if you have studied yourself by trying to match your emotions to appropriate ways of allowing your body to move, you have all of the ingredients required to make up a proper response to a spontaneous attack. By all means, learn the strikes and immobilizations in the book. But be free in applying them, any piece of them, or, most importantly, the principles that make them work. With time you will understand that it is only important that you are safe and sound at the end of the fracas. How it happens is not as important as the end result.

4
Grappling with a Stick

The title of this chapter is a little misleading. I am sure that you don't really need to learn how to grapple with a stick. Sticks are rarely adversarial in and of themselves. What we *do* need to explore are some strategies, principles, and tricks for grappling with another person *over* a stick. Therefore, the following section will be devoted to things that can happen at very close quarters when a stick is involved.

As usual, you must realize that you are tussling with a human being in these situations, so I must remind you *not* to fixate on the stick, but on the whole person. Don't forget that you can still punch, kick, throw, bite, and scream, even though you will be dealing with stick-oriented scenarios.

Another reminder: I can only present strategies here. The principles are *illustrated* by the techniques. Memorizing the rote technique will limit your real self-defense capability. The chances are slim that the attack that happens to you will be identical to any of the scenarios in this book. To drive that point home, I want to start right off by demonstrating a simple disarm that hardly involves the stick at all. The secret of this technique lies almost entirely with the legs and foot-work. See if you can duplicate it.

Grappling Technique 1:
Two-Handed Disarm

Two people are grappling over the stick. The defender
bends his knees and then lifts the stick as he walks
forward. The assailant is toppled when the defender
turns and executes a hip throw.

This technique is about as straightforward as they
get. The principle behind it is quite profound, however.
If you could feel the defender's arms, you would see
that the muscles are not being used to wrench the stick
out of the attacker's hand. The legs, distancing, and
timing do the work. As you practice, if you find yourself
wrestling with the other person, STOP. Instead, work on
developing a smooth, flowing movement. Experiment
with the angle at which you move forward, start with a
45-degree angle, and adjust.

Grappling Technique 2:
Defense Against a One-Hand Grab
From the shizen, the defender responds against a grab
of the arm by moving back at a 45-degree angle and
lifting and placing the stick against the wrist of the
assailant. Follow up with an arm bar if the attacker
holds on, with a strike if he or she lets go.

The footwork is an essential part of this grappling
technique. If the defender grabs the stick the opposite
way or grabs the wrist, the principles are the same.
Experiment and find the adjustments that need to be
made.

63

Grappling Technique 3:
Defense Against a Two-Hand Grab

The attacker grabs the stick with both hands. In this scenario one hand is between the defender's hands, one outside. The defender attacks the assailant's inside hand with his thumb at the fork of the ring and little fingers. The defender simultaneously crushes the attacker's thumb against the stick with the other hand. The defender easily pulls away from the attacker, who is all too willing to let go at this point. A follow-up strike may or may not be necessary.

This last technique should be performed with a firm or committed attitude. Often it is the intention of the defender that becomes translated into pain for the attacker. In that way, this last defense is much more than a technique.

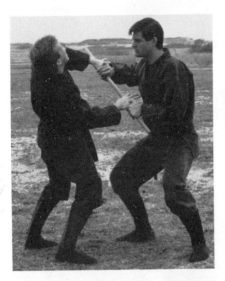
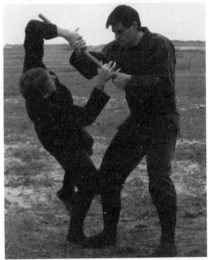
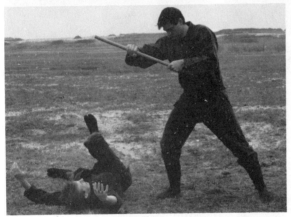
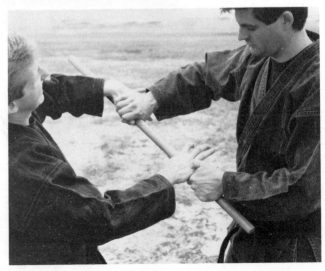

65 Richton Public Library

Grappling Technique 4:
Defense Against a Two-Hand Grab
The attacker grabs the stick as before, and the defender makes a darting motion to the eyes and then slips his arm under the attacker's for a lock and throw.

The main points to remember about this technique are: move your body in for the throw, don't try to pull the attacker toward you. Lock the arm as shown, don't shoulder wrestle. Twist and throw with a naturally erect posture, do not bend over at the waist.

67

Grappling Technique 5:
Defense Against a Two-Hand Grab
The assailant grabs the stick as before, and the defender
uses the right elbow to weigh down the attacker's left
arm. The defender then reaches around the attacker's
head to grab the other end of the stick for the choke.

This last technique is extremely dangerous. I almost
deleted it from the book. Please take care, and remember: your training partner is going to do it to you
next.

Some of the techniques above are rather exotic, but they contain certain fundamentals of taijutsu that are best illustrated in context. The most important of them is the principle that reminds us to *not* wrestle with the person. Stomp on the foot or knee, rap on the soft back of the attacker's hands with your knuckles, punch the attacker in the head as his or her hands grip the stick, or let go of the stick and fight the whole person. These are all preferable to wrestling options, as are the ones that you can come up with yourself based on an intelligent strategy and the principles of taijutsu.

We have also assumed that the attacker has grabbed *your* stick, which you were wielding in your own self-defense. It is very likely that you have grabbed *the assailant's* stick and need to disarm him or her. Keep all these possibilities in mind. Chapter 6 deals with un-armed defense against a stick. Obviously, these two chapters go hand in hand.

5
The Staff and Short Stick

T he principles of taijutsu apply to fighting with the long and very short stick. You will have to exaggerate the taijutsu with a long stick and be careful to use taijutsu in spite of the size of the short one.

In the Kukishin ryu, there are many long staff waza that one can memorize to gain proficiency. They are not appropriately within the scope of this book, but I want to mention that they exist.

While it is not discrete to walk around with a six-foot staff, there are many contingency weapons—such as a shovel or rake—with which you may have to improvise. As mentioned before, if you intend to study the various combat systems that make up Bujinkan Ninjutsu as an art, the staff and short stick must be included. This section is merely an introduction to the characteristics of both of these useful weapons and how they might be used for fighting.

Here are three common attitudes for the long staff:

1. Shizen no kamae
2. Hira ichimonji no kamae
3. Ichimonji no kamae

1

2

3

Using the nine strikes we practiced in Chapter 2, notice the difference in weight between the hanbo and bo. Compensate by becoming more aware of the need for effective taijutsu. Do not try to "muscle" the stick. Here are some suggestions for initiating a strike from each of the three attitudes. I will leave it to the reader to practice the other striking angles/directions.

Continued on next page . . .

Now try this short waza. It is a variation of one that is taught in Kukishin ryu.

The short stick can be used in two ways: striking and grappling.

1. Attack vital points, such as neck or chest.
2. Use when grappling, for example, against the wrist or elbow.

Continued on next page . . .

Use the short stick to attack the neck or chest for the surest defense.

If using the short stick for grappling, the attacker's wrists or elbows are good targets.

Admittedly, this section on long and short sticks is
rather cursory. This does not mean that I feel that this
kind of training is unimportant, but merely too advanced and involved to go into while still being true to
the theme of this book.

At the present time it seems that advanced stick
training is studied seriously by students who have
attained a godan or fifth-degree belt. I do not think that
the instructors are being elitist, I think they merely
recognize that the study of Kukishin ryu, as an art, is
time-consuming and seems to fit naturally into the
training evolution at this level of ability. This definitely
does not mean that one must wait until fourth dan to
pick up a long bo, only that the practitioner must be
patient before he or she can expect to master this rich
tradition.

If one were to wait until fifth dan to get familiariza-
tion with these weapons, it is quite unlikely that a true
facility would be gained in this lifetime. So, work with
these weapons, by all means, but have fun and don't be
too hard on yourself.

Also, be sure to address the contingency of your own
practical self-defense. Try the strikes with a shovel,
umbrella, rake, or anything else that resembles a stick.
Use your whole body to hit, as always.

Try the short stick techniques with a pen or fork. Use
your imagination. In accordance with the theme of this
book, you can probably expect *not* to have your favorite
weapon with you if you are attacked.

Ninja weapons, by the way, were devised from everyday articles from the corresponding historical era. It is
humorous to think that, 500 years from now, there may
be a Bic pen belonging to a present day ninja in a
museum someplace. It is also quite possible.

6
Unarmed Against the Stick

Although the preceding chapters of this book were a necessary introduction to stick fighting, this particular chapter may be the most useful and important for real life. With few exceptions, people do not feel comfortable walking around carrying a stick. Most of us must worry, instead, about the possibility of being attacked by a person who has a stick and means to harm us with it.

The secret to avoiding the striking stick involves two strategies:

Strategy 1: be too far away to get hit.

Strategy 2: be too close to be hit.

Your taijutsu must be smooth through the hips. You must remember to take small (yes, small) steps.

Fortunately, most of the attacks that you will encounter in the West are of the "baseball–homerun variety." As we discussed before, this is a rather inefficient method of striking. We will be exploiting this inefficiency in the following technique section.

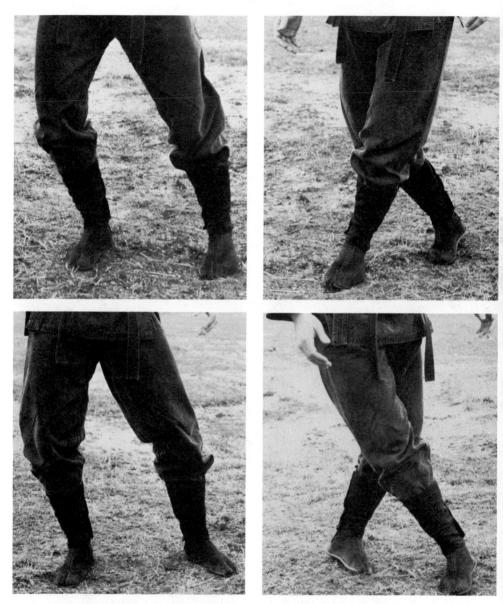

To be more complete, we will also deal with several other striking methods that one might encounter; of course it would be impossible to include all possibilities here.

Unarmed Technique 1:
Too Far Away

The attacker swings at the head of the defender, who glides away out of range. (Please notice that the defender does not hop back—rather, he moves through the hips in a variation of the taijutsu fundamental illustrated.) Before the assailant can resume the attack, the defender has glided back in and attacked the arm with the left fist. He then grasps over and under both arms for an arm bar to throw the attacker over his left leg.

This is not the most comfortable technique to perform. Once you are out of the way, you may get the compulsion to just keep going. This might, indeed, be the thing to do. On the other hand, you may be merely postponing the inevitable. This technique does not allow the attacker to strike again. With practice, you will get more comfortable with the distancing. Practice *slowly* and then speed up *very* gradually. Remember, this exercise is for practicing how *not* to get hit. Get that part of the training down pat from the very beginning.

Unarmed Technique 2:
Too Close
As the attacker attempts a similar attack, the defender uses small, quick steps to move inside the arc of the swing. This time he grasps under the arms to set up for the throw and disarm.

It goes without saying that it goes against the grain to move *into* a stick attack. Again, start slowly so that you may learn without fear. If you can assimilate the necessary timing, distance, and, most importantly, the rhythm or "breath" of this strategy, it is ridiculously easy to move past the attacker.

89

Unarmed Technique 3:
Defense Against an Overhead Strike
The attacker strikes straight down at the head of the
defender who lowers himself below and inside the path
of the stick while punching up under the attacker's chin.
The defender then executes an elbow immobilization
with the right arm and relieves the attacker of his stick.

This last technique is a variation of a muto dori
sword disarm. If performed with great precision it will
work against a sharp sword.

Unarmed Technique 4:
Defense Against a Poke
The attacker pokes to the midsection of the defender, who disappears to the right side of the assailant. The defender then pushes the stick to the ground and steps on it to trap the attacker's hands.

The above technique works only because of the knee action.

Unarmed Technique 5:
Defense Against a Back-Handed Strike

The attacker swings back-handed at the defender, who moves in and strikes the arm with the left fist. Stepping under the arm, he effects a throw.

95

While running the risk of becoming repetitive, I must emphasize how important it is to understand the rhythm of the attack and to blend with it. Most humans have a fear of a fast-swung stick, which probably dates back to prehistoric days. I think that it is a healthy fear, but one that is easily overcome by applied reason. There were many solutions to freezing to death in a cave under a bearskin. Use the same brain power that built the two-story colonial with hot water baseboard heating to solve this prehistoric problem. Then act! The danger stays the same, the fear lessens.

I am afraid to say too much about the subject of avoiding that first strike. It is a simple formula:

1. Understand the strategies and taijutsu required.
2. Believe that you deserve to be, and can be, safe.
3. Move.

Period.

7
The Stick Fight

You are casually raking leaves on an autumn afternoon. The sky is blue and there is a slight brittleness to the air that reminds you that winter is just around the corner. How wonderful, you think, to be out and alive on a day like this. You work lazily, enjoying the mild exercise and testing your senses. You feel the dry rake handle in your hands. You aren't used to raking, so you wonder if the blisters will come. There is a lingering smell of burning leaves in the neighborhood. There is the crackling sound of the leaves you are raking. And the snarl of a dog . . .

You look up to see a vicious pit bull charging straight for you. Petrified, you swat at the beast with your rake and bolt for your front door. The dog grabs your pant leg and you feel that you may be knocked to the ground. You stop momentarily and try to shake loose; no use. You hit the dog again, this time with the hard end of the stick. He backs off for only a second, bares his teeth, and begins to leap at your face. Now what?

I can't tell you!

You see, only you can know what to do. Only you are there. Only you know the distancing, the timing, the emotional impact of the attack, the distance to the door, the size of the pit bull, your own capabilities, etc., etc., etc.

If we are to continue to use the model that we have been employing up to now, we would have to admit that this scenario is devoid of all of the other easily categorized components that we worked with in the strategy chapter. And that, my fellow warrior aspirants, is life. Any training method is merely that: a training method. Even the training method in this book is useful only if you try to apply it directly to real life. Only the things that you learn from working with the method are useful. Remember, learn from the techniques, learn from the methods; don't just imitate movements. A fight will *never* look, much less feel, like a training exercise. So why do them, you might ask? Why not spar with people and try to imitate a real fight? Good question.

Here is my opinion. The very things that are forbidden so that sparring or full-contact fighting is reasonably safe and civilized are the very things that are most necessary for understanding the true nature of combat. Sparring either becomes a complicated game of tag where people get hurt by mistake, or an emotionless dance devoid of anything practical for real life. Full-contact fighting demonstrates the courage and stamina of the human animal, but the tactics employed are those of a game rather than of a life-and-death situation.

ENLIGHTENED COMBAT

About 800 years ago a man by the name of Daisuke Nishina (later Diasuke Togakure) joined a local leader in a battle against the forces of the oppressive Heike government. After a conflict which lasted several years, the resistance movement was crushed and Daisuke barely escaped with his life. I have to admit that this was not a very auspicious beginning to the Togakure ryu, but it is the birth of a centuries-old tradition for surviving overwhelming odds.

Daisuke was a very smart man. He took the lessons he learned and began to create methods of teaching his descendants how to prevail in life-or-death situations. For the next 33 generations, additions and modifications were incorporated by other survivors of a thousand other battles. Records were kept secretly, as the study of combat tactics, during certain historical periods, were forbidden to the ordinary Japanese citizen and reserved for the samurai elite. But records were kept nonetheless. Today, the essence of what allows a ninja to survive has evolved to the level of an art: Ninpo, the art of the invisible warrior. By decision of the 34th Soke of the Togakure ryu, Masaaki Hatsumi,

Continued on next page . . .

101

certain aspects of the training method are no longer a secret. They are available for anyone who has the understanding, the desire, and the commitment to learn. This training method allows the student to absorb the lessons of 800 years in a relatively safe environment. It is unique in my experience.

This method is not designed to make you the heavyweight champion of the world. It is designed to teach you how to be safe in a crazy world, and more than that. It teaches the individual how to exercise his or her personal, "unalienable" rights with the subtlety that keeps him or her safe from those parasites who live by usurping the rights of others. And it teaches the gentleness that makes the life of the benevolent warrior a joy to other productive individuals around him.

It is said that the eyes are the key to the soul. The most terrifying eyes I have ever seen belong to Masaaki Hatsumi. The most innocent eyes I have ever seen in a grown man belong to Masaaki Hatsumi. Strangely, there is no contradiction. He is a ninja.

Anyone who would attack you is wrong. Turn their terrifying ignorance back upon them. Man without reason is the devil. Train yourself to move as a rational person. Use the methods in this book to help you understand how your body really can work to make yourself safe as long as you are in the right.

I wouldn't insult your intelligence by saying something like: wish yourself safe and it will come true. This is not the way of the warrior. I will not exhort you to do something, anything. You will probably do the wrong thing. I will not even bet that you could think yourself out of the problem. Ignorance in numbers can overcome rational men.

You must do all of these things.

People are confronted with incredible, irrational violence every day. I believe that it is a result of a lack of philosophy—a vacuum where logic is supposed to be. That is why the rational person can be very powerful.

I live in a place where the military, the police, and the courts are a rather effective deterrent to utter chaos and mayhem. Yet, the danger exists, and will probably always exist. You and I are ultimately responsible for our own protection. With that unalienable right comes a commensurate responsibility to know what we are doing.

When the attack comes you must be emotionally, intellectually, and physically prepared to do the appropriate thing. It is literally a microcosm of the larger battle between the rational and the irrational in humans. The irrational can win only by default, but it wins all too often.

Which still leaves us our problem with the dog. I have to admit that there is no special **Technique 23: Defense Against a Pit Bull.**

Just remember, humans keep pit bulls as pets, tigers in cages, sharks in fish tanks. How? We wanted to. We figured out how to do it. And we did it.

Afterword

T his book is for instructional purposes only. The author and publisher accept no responsibility for the use or misuse of any of the techniques or material presented in this volume.

Taijutsu is a body flow which cannot be adequately illustrated in a static photo sequence. Readers interested in learning Ninpo taijutsu from a qualified instructor should contact:

The Warrior Information Network
3067 East Waterloo Road
Stockton, California 95205

About the Author

Jack Hoban is a long-time practitioner of the martial arts and a former U.S. Marine Corps Captain. His name is usually associated with the Japanese martial philosophy of Ninpo, in which he holds a Shidoshi license from Grandmaster Masaaki Hatsumi. He also has a close personal association with Stephen K. Hayes, the Western world's foremost authority on the ninja.

Although he teaches occasional seminars across the country and leads a taijutsu club in his own area, Hoban refers to himself as a practitioner rather than a teacher. He holds a master's degree in business administration and is an executive in the marketing department of a major financial services corporation. He is married and does not have a pit bull for a pet.

Index